ON THE WAY
TO THE MOON

by Becky Gold

Modern Curriculum Press
Parsippany, New Jersey

Credits

Photos: All photos © Pearson Learning unless otherwise noted. Front & back cover: NASA. Title page: NASA. 5: t. NASA; b. ©John Bova/Science Source/Photo Researchers, Inc. 7: UCO/Lick Observatory Photo. 8: Mike Boyatt/AGStock. 9: The Granger Collection, NY. 10: t. The Granger Collection, NY; b. Special Collections, Vassar College Libraries, Poughkeepsie, NY. 11: NASA. 12: t. NASA; b.l. The Granger Collection, NY; m.b.; b.r. Archive Photos. 13: b.l. Silver Burdett Ginn; b.r. AP/Wide World. 14, 15, 16: NASA. 17: t. NASA; b. Richard Cummins/Corbis. 19: UCO/Lick Observatory Photos. 21: Tony Stone Images. 22–23: Ron Dahlquist/Tony Stone Images. 24: NASA. 25: t. NASA; b. Neal Peters Collection. 26: l.; m. NASA; r. Archive Photos. 27, 28, 29, 30, 31, 32, 33, 34, 35: NASA. 36: Jerry Lodriguss. 37, 38, 39, 40, 41, 42, 43, 44, 45, 46, 47: NASA.
Illustrations: 20: Gary Torrisi.
Title Page: Astronaut Edwin E. Aldrin Jr. steps onto the moon's surface from the Apollo II Lunar Module.

Cover and book design by Liz Kril

Modern Curriculum Press
An imprint of Pearson Learning
299 Jefferson Road, P.O. Box 480
Parsippany, NJ 07054–0480

www.pearsonlearning.com

1-800-321-3106

ISBN 0-7652-0896-2

6 7 8 9 10 11 12 13   MA   07 06 05 04 03 02 01

Modern
Curriculum
Press

CONTENTS

Chapter 1
MOON STORIES

Many hundreds of years ago, long before there were ships that could travel in space, the moon was a mystery to people on the earth. What was that glowing ball that came out at night? Why did it keep getting smaller, then larger? Why didn't it fall from the sky?

An astronomer gets a close-up look at the moon through a telescope.

For as long as there have been people on the earth, there have been questions about the moon. Through the ages, people have tried to come up with answers.

To the native people of Bolivia (buh LIHV-ee uh), in South America, the moon was a great chief who once lived on the earth. The Abaluyia (ah bah LOO yah) people of Kenya, in Africa, believed the moon and the sun were brothers who fought in the sky. The ancient Egyptians connected the moon to a cat goddess named Bast. Both the cat's eyes and the moon shone in the night.

In other parts of the world, people believed they saw different pictures in the moon. The Haida (HYE dah) Indians of Canada saw a woman carrying a bucket. The ancient Greeks saw a goddess they named Selene (sih LEE nee) in a silver chariot. The Chinese saw a toad. In the more recent past, people have had fun looking for the face of the "Man in the Moon" on bright moonlit nights.

Close-up of the
full moon in
the night sky

A farmer harvests wheat under the harvest moon.

People in the past have also used the moon to mark time as a kind of calendar. In fact, in some languages, the word for *moon* meant "month." A Native American nation called the Sioux (soo) made a calendar of 13 moons, or months. Each moon had a name, such as Moon of Black Cherries, Moon of Green Corn, and Moon of Severe Cold.

The moon that shines in the fall, or autumn, is called the harvest moon. It has been special to farmers throughout the ages. Because it is so big and bright, it gives enough light for people to work until late in the day, bringing in crops.

Even though people of the past found the moon to be helpful, mysterious, and interesting, they did not know much about it. They only knew what they could see with their own eyes.

Then one night, almost 400 years ago, someone got a closer look at the moon. An Italian scientist named Galileo Galilei built a telescope that was more powerful than any telescope made before. It had two pieces of glass set into the ends of a tube. By looking through the glass, objects in the distance looked larger.

Galileo decided to take his new instrument outside at night to look at the moon. When he gazed through the glass, he saw something wonderful.

Galileo demonstrates his new telescope.

Early astronomers view the sky with different instruments.

Maria Mitchell was the first woman astronomer in the United States. She discovered a comet in 1847.

Galileo saw that the moon had a rough, bumpy surface. It was not the smooth, shiny ball it looked like from the earth. He discovered that the brighter places were mostly hills and mountains. The flat areas were lower, which is why they appeared darker. Galileo named the flat areas *maria*, which means "seas." Even though scientists now know there were never any oceans on the moon, the name *seas* remained.

As more people saw the moon through telescopes, they discovered more about it. They saw there were never any clouds. The view was always clear. They realized that this must mean there was little or no air on the moon. Because there was no air, people also decided that the moon must be very hot where the sun shone. It would be very cold where the sun didn't shine. Yet, people still had much to learn about the moon.

Moon Closeup

Have you ever heard about something happening "once in a blue moon"? Every few years there are two full moons in one month. The second full moon is called a blue moon. The moon can also look blue if the earth's atmosphere is full of dust from a volcano. Seeing a blue moon is very rare. So an event said to happen once in a blue moon is rare, too.

Chapter 2
MOON DISCOVERIES

In the 400 years since Galileo's discoveries, bigger and better telescopes and other instruments have helped scientists learn many things about the moon. They know that the moon is as hot as 260 degrees Fahrenheit (FER un hyt) in the sunny parts. It is as cold as minus 273 degrees Fahrenheit in the shaded areas.

They have learned that the moon is about 240,000 miles away from the earth. This means that if there were a road to the moon, it would take six months to drive there at 55 miles per hour.

1608

1671

1780

Two of Galileo's telescopes

Sir Isaac Newton's reflecting telescope

Sir William Herschel's Great Telescope

The moon is about one fourth the size of the earth. If the earth were the size of a soccer ball, the moon would be the size of a softball.

The moon makes no light of its own. People can see the moon because it reflects the sun's light. The sunlight shining on the moon makes it look as though it is shining by itself.

Scientists now know the moon goes around, or orbits, the earth once every 27 days and 8 hours. They also know that both the earth and the moon travel around the sun.

Not only does the moon orbit the sun, it also spins on its axis, the same way the earth does. However, it spins only once as it goes around the earth. Because of this, people can see only one side of the moon.

1997

1997

A home telescope

The Hubble Space
Telescope

13

Linda Tyler, Nancy L. Trent, and Sandra Richards view the rock brought back from the moon by *Apollo 14.*

Scientists finally got to touch and look at pieces of the moon after astronauts who landed on the moon brought back rocks. These rocks are among the oldest rocks scientists have ever studied. The rocks tell that the moon is about 4.6 billion years old.

Some of the rocks are made of basalt, which is a kind of rock that makes up much of the ocean floor. Other moon rocks are not like any rocks on the earth.

14

The moon has gravity, too, but much less than the earth. Gravity is a natural force that acts like a great magnet. It gives things their weight. Gravity also allows people to walk on the earth without floating into space!

If someone weighs 100 pounds on the earth, he or she would weigh only 17 pounds on the moon. Each step that person would take on the moon would be a giant step! The weight of the astronauts' spacesuits on the moon helped to keep them from bouncing too high when they walked.

Spacesuit worn on the moon by astronaut Neil Armstrong

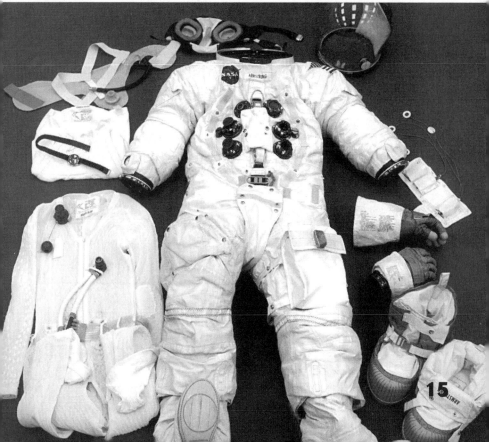

Neil Armstrong was the first human to walk on the moon. The year was 1969. When he took his first step, he said, "That's one small step for man, one giant leap for mankind!" Because no one owns the moon, it is something people from all

Apollo II **commander Neil Armstrong**

countries can explore. Like looking through Galileo's telescope, whatever is learned about the moon can be shared with everyone.

moon Closeup

Scientists have had different ideas about where the moon came from. The latest idea is that long ago the earth was hit by a small planet. Parts of the earth and the planet were broken and thrown into space. The pieces came together to make the moon.

Chapter 3
THE MOON'S MYSTERIES

People long ago asked many questions about the moon. One question was, why does the moon appear to grow smaller and then larger again every month?

Long ago, people made up stories about the moon changing shape every month. They used what they knew about life on the earth. The native people of Bolivia believed that when the moon was dark, it was off hunting. When it came back from the hunt, its face was dirty. Every day the moon would wash a part of its face until its face was clean and the moon was full again. It then let its face become dirtier each day until it went hunting again.

A crescent moon appears over the desert.

People now know why the moon slowly appears to get smaller bit by bit, then grows larger again every month. Scientists have seen that the moon moves every day on its path, or orbit, around the earth. This causes the sun's rays to hit the moon's surface in a different way each day.

Because of the moon's movement, and because the moon reflects the sun's light, the moon looks like it changes shape each day. These changes are called the moon's phases.

The moon takes about a month to complete one orbit around the earth. During this time, the moon goes through eight phases. When the sun is shining on the moon's far side, which is the side we never see, the phase is called the new moon. During the new moon phase, we cannot see the moon at all!

The moon then waxes, or gets bigger, until it looks like a full circle. When the moon looks like a full circle, it is called the full moon. Then the moon gets smaller, or wanes, until it is the new moon again.

The beginning of the moon's cycle of phases is the new moon. By the time the moon is full, it is halfway through its monthly phases. The moon begins to wane as the sunlit side turns away from us. The half moon looks like a backwards "D." A thin, crescent shape is the last part of the moon we see before the new moon. Then the phases start all over again.

Sometimes it seems as though the full moon fades or disappears in a short period of time. Long ago, many people believed that some kind of monster was eating the moon. The Cherokee said that a big frog was eating the moon. They would make loud noises to frighten the frog away.

Today people know that the moon fades because of an eclipse. The moon rotates around the earth. Both the moon and the earth rotate around the sun. As they do, sometimes all three bodies line up in a straight line. This causes an eclipse.

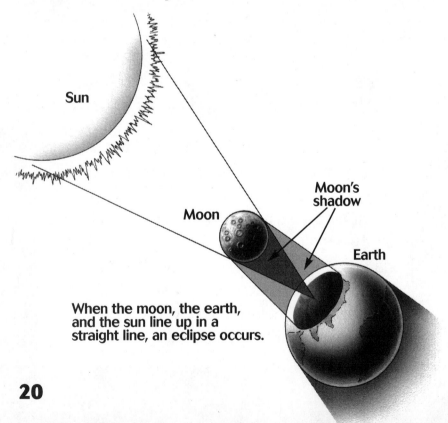

Sun

Moon

Moon's shadow

Earth

When the moon, the earth, and the sun line up in a straight line, an eclipse occurs.

Partial lunar eclipse

A lunar eclipse happens when the earth moves between the moon and the sun. The earth blocks the sun's light from reaching the moon. The lunar eclipse is total when the moon moves into the darkest part of the earth's shadow. The eclipse is partial if the moon is only partly in the earth's shadow.

During an eclipse, the moon may seem to fade and turn a red or rusty color. At other times, the lighted part of the moon gets smaller and smaller.

When the moon passes between the earth and the sun, the eclipse is called a solar eclipse. At that time the sun seems to disappear. The sky becomes darker, and the temperature drops. It might seem as though the sun has set and it is almost evening.

Lunar eclipses are more common than solar eclipses. Long ago, people became much more frightened when the sun seemed to disappear in the middle of the day than when the moon faded away at night. Some people would shoot arrows tipped with fire into the sky to "relight" the sun.

Another mystery that scientists have solved is how the moon affects the ocean tides on the earth. The tides are the daily rise and fall of the oceans along the coastlines. Every 12 hours the ocean rises and covers the beach. After 6 hours the water falls back and more of the beach can be seen once again.

The ocean's tides are caused by the moon's gravity pulling on the earth. The water in the ocean that is closest to the moon bulges out toward the moon. As that part of the earth spins away from the moon, the water goes down.

The moon's gravity causes the ocean tides on the earth.

23

Some moon mysteries were solved long ago. Over 2,000 years ago, the ancient Greeks were the ones who figured out that the moon's light comes from the sun's light. Other mysteries had to wait to be solved until scientists had bigger and better telescopes to study the moon.

However, the more scientists learned, the more questions they had. The only way they could answer their questions was somehow to get closer to the moon.

Moon Closeup

The greatest range of tides in the world happens in the Bay of Fundy in Canada. Every six hours the water level may go up or down as much as 60 feet. Think of three giraffes standing on each other's head. That's how high the tides get.

Chapter 4
TARGET: MOON

In ancient times a Greek writer told the story of a man who tied the wings of an eagle and the wings of a vulture to his shoulders. He then flew to the moon. From there, he said that people on the earth looked like ants!

Back then, people could only make up stories about going to the moon. They did not know how to send a spaceship to the moon.

Elliott (Henry Thomas) and E.T. ride across the full moon in the movie "E.T.–The Extra-Terrestrial."

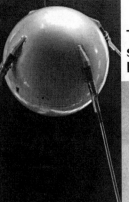

The second Russian satellite *Sputnik II* is launched in 1957. ▼

▲ Full-scale model of first Russian satellite *Sputnik I*

Over 40 years ago, both the Soviet Union (now Russia) and the United States started on the long journey to send people to the moon. Scientists learned that a spaceship needed a powerful launcher, or rocket, to thrust, or push, the spaceship into orbit. With reverse thrusters, a spaceship could return to the earth.

▲ The United States' first satellite, *Explorer 1,* is prepared for launching in 1958.

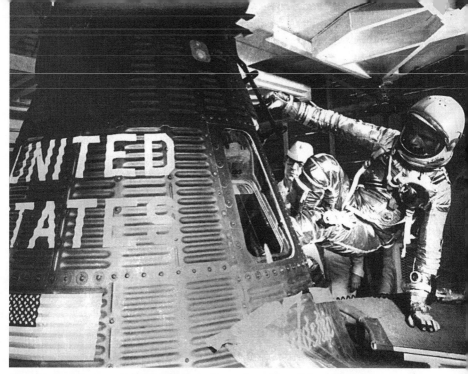

Mercury astronaut John Glenn, Jr., enters the *Friendship 7* space capsule.

By 1961, NASA (National Aeronautics and Space Administration) began the *Mercury* space program. On May 5, Alan Shepard took a 15-minute flight into space. The following year, John Glenn, Jr. became the first U.S. astronaut to orbit the earth.

In 1965, the Soviet Union sent Alexei Leonov into space. Leonov was the first person to take a walk in space by leaving his capsule.

Shortly after Alexei Leonov walked in space, Ed White became the first American to do the same. The space race was on!

Since the moon is the earth's closest neighbor, it was the place space-program scientists wanted to explore. In space terms, 250,000 miles is not that far!

The moon was perfect for other reasons, too. Unmanned spacecraft had been sending back pictures and information about the moon since 1959. These spacecraft discovered that the moon was not too hot for a spacecraft to land on. It also had a flat surface. Scientists felt they knew enough about spacecraft and the moon to send people there safely.

One of the first photos of the moon taken from an unmanned spaceship

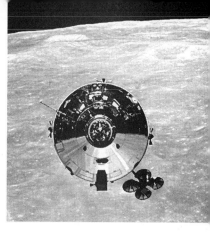

Apollo 10 **orbits above the moon's surface.**

The first step was to travel to the moon and back safely without landing. With astronauts aboard, the American spacecraft *Apollo 7* and *Apollo 9* orbited the earth. In 1968, *Apollo 8* left the earth, flew to the moon, and made 10 orbits around it. The next year, *Apollo 10* flew to the moon and came within eight miles of the moon's surface. The next step was to actually land on the moon.

Moon Closeup

NASA chose some of the names of their space programs from ancient myths. Mercury was the Roman messenger of the gods. Apollo was a Greek god known for being a swift runner.

29

Chapter 5
LANDING ON THE MOON

On July 16, 1969, NASA launched the spacecraft *Apollo 11*. In it were three astronauts: Commander Neil Armstrong, Lunar Module Pilot Edwin Aldrin, and Command Module Pilot Michael Collins. They were headed for the moon. This time the spacecraft would not just circle the moon. It would land.

After four days, *Apollo 11* reached the moon. While the command module orbited the moon, Armstrong and Aldrin flew a smaller spacecraft called the *Eagle* to the moon's surface. On July 20, 1969, almost everyone in the United States was watching television. People wanted to see the astronauts take the first moonwalk.

After stepping onto the moon, astronauts Armstrong and Aldrin planted the American flag on the surface.

Footprint on the moon

The footprints the astronauts left on the moon may still be there a million years from now. This is because there is no air on the moon. So there is no wind to blow the dust around.

Air also carries sound waves. Without air, sound can't travel. This makes the moon silent. Sound could not be heard even when the astronauts were breaking rocks!

Astronaut Edwin E. Aldrin Jr. drives a core tube into the lunar soil.

While on the moon, the astronauts were busy. They took pictures of everything. They collected rocks to bring back for scientists to study. They drilled holes in the moon's surface to see what was under it.

From the astronaut's work, scientists were given a very good look at the surface of the moon. They saw that it has thousands of craters. A crater looks like a round pit. It is ring-shaped with a small rim. A crater's floor is lower than the land outside the rim.

Many of the moon's craters were caused by huge rocks, called meteors, crashing onto the surface from outer space. Some of the craters may have been caused by pieces of comets hitting the surface. A comet is a large ball of ice, rock, and frozen gases.

Besides craters, there are also mountains, valleys, and flat lands on the moon's surface. The valleys were formed by liquid rock that flowed from volcanoes when the moon was still hot inside.

In 1971, astronauts took hundreds of tree seeds to the moon. When they returned to earth, they gave seedlings that grew from these seeds to people all over the world. These "moon trees" remind everyone of the Apollo program.

NASA sent Apollo spacecraft to the moon until 1972. The last astronauts who visited the moon left a falcon feather and a four-leaf clover on the surface. They also left a marker showing the history of moon travel.

The moon's surface is covered with craters.

A model of the *Surveyor A* **satellite, which is a lunar soft lander**

Although NASA no longer sent people to the moon, they did continue to send instruments. Included were probes to collect moon samples and cameras to take pictures.

Russia and Japan also sent probes and unmanned lunar landers to the moon. In 1998, scientists got the biggest surprise of all! They found something that was not supposed to be on the moon at all.

Moon Closeup

One of the Apollo moon flights never landed. On the way to the moon, an oxygen tank broke on *Apollo 13.* **The astronauts managed to go all the way around the moon and back to the earth in their crippled spacecraft.**

Chapter 6
THE BONE-DRY MOON

The Apollo astronauts brought 842 pounds (382 kilograms) of moon rock and dirt back to the earth. When scientists examined the rocks and dirt, they found no water in any of the samples.

Thousands of pictures were taken of the moon. In these pictures no one could find any marks on the surface that could have been made by flowing water. As a result, scientists believed there was no water on the moon.

A photograph taken of moon mountains by astronauts on *Apollo 17*

The Hale-Bopp comet streaks across the sky.

However, scientists did know that over millions of years, pieces of meteors and comets had hit or passed close by the moon. The comet pieces most likely had water in them.

Where would the water go after a comet hit the moon's surface? Much of it would have immediately evaporated, or turned to gas on the surface. Yet some scientists thought that some of the water ended up as ice in the areas of the moon that are always dark and cold. These areas are deep in craters at the moon's north pole and south pole.

To test their thinking, scientists sent a spacecraft called *Clementine* to the moon in 1996. Instruments on the *Clementine* sent radio waves to the north and south poles. The radio waves told the scientists there might be ice under the dark areas of the moon.

Although most of the dark areas get a little sunlight, some parts do not. These areas are called cold traps. For 2 billion years, the cold traps have stayed at minus 280 degrees Fahrenheit. At this very cold temperature, they might have collected the ice left by comets and meteors.

An artist's picture of the *Clementine* **spacecraft**

The information from *Clementine* still did not say for sure that there was ice on the moon. So a spacecraft called the *Lunar Prospector* was sent to orbit the moon in January 1998. *Prospector* found hydrogen, which could mean water ice.

Some scientists believe there could be 10 million to 300 million tons of frozen water in the cold traps of the moon. This is 2.6 billion to 26 billion gallons. The ice is like frost mixed in with the soil.

NASA's *Lunar Prospector*

The news that there is ice on the moon suggests all kinds of ideas. Some scientists believe enough water could be made from ice on the moon to start a small human colony. Scientists also have been thinking of other ways moon water could be used in the future.

Moon Closeup

Even though the moon's ice cannot be seen as ice, some cartoonists have thought about what water on the moon might mean. Some are even drawing cartoons showing land on the moon that is next to a lake.

Chapter 7
Living on the Moon

Water is made up of two elements, hydrogen and oxygen. Hydrogen and oxygen are very important to human life and to space travel. Mixed together one way, they make water, which is needed for life. Mixed together another way, they make rocket fuel.

Some day astronauts may refill the tanks on their spacecraft with fuel made on the moon.

If rocket fuel could be made from the ice found on the moon, then spaceships could be launched from the moon. There could even be "filling stations" on the moon. Rockets could be filled with fuel made there. Then fuel would not have to be carried from the earth. Some scientists say that there could be enough water on the moon to make fuel for one million launches of the space shuttle!

A cutout view, including gardens, of how astronauts might live on the moon

The oxygen found in water could also be used to make air for breathing. The hydrogen in the water could be used to grow plants. All of these ideas have caused scientists to believe that people could live on the moon.

Besides ice in the cold traps of the moon, there is always sunlight on some high crater rims. From this sunlight, scientists could get solar power. Having both power and water on the moon means that people would be able to live there all the time. But what would people who lived there do?

An artist's idea of what a lunar outpost might look like

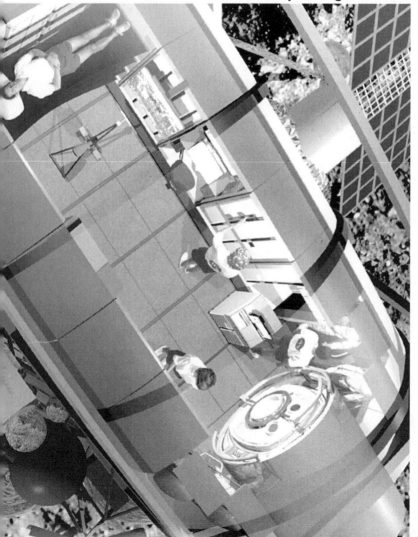

One thing moon dwellers could do is organize missions to go further out into space. Perhaps they could build spaceships on the moon that would be sent to Mars.

These spaceships might even be able to explore further in space. The moon could become a "stepping stone" for exploring the rest of the solar system.

The Sojourner probe on Mars

Moon ice might also contain clues to the moon's past. Scientists believe that when comet and meteor pieces hit the moon, water in them could have formed layers that could be studied. The ice would be like a 2-billion-year time line. It would tell the history of what happened to the cold traps where the ice is stored. Also, the water may have come from far out in space. It might tell scientists more about those distant places.

An artist's idea of future industries on the moon

In the future the moon might also become a place where things are made. Studies of rocks brought back by astronauts show that the moon does have many useful building materials. These materials include ores such as aluminum, titanium, nickel, magnesium, and uranium.

View of the earth from the moon

With all the ideas of what could be done on the moon, people living there would be so busy they would have no time to miss the earth. They would be doing something no one else had done before. And maybe, like Galileo looking at the moon, they would sometimes look at the earth and say, "I wonder what is going on there?"

Moon Closeup

There is another valuable element on the moon. It is called helium 3. On the earth, helium 3 is very rare. When it is combined with hydrogen, it creates a lot of energy. This energy could replace energy made by nuclear power and oil.

GLOSSARY

astronaut (ah STROH naht) a pilot or crew member of a spacecraft

axis (AK sihs) a real or imaginary line through an object such as a planet or a moon, about which the object spins

comet (KAH mit) a body in space made of frozen ice and dust that shines brightly and forms a long tail when it approaches the sun

crater (KRAYT ur) a round pit or hollow shaped like a bowl on the surface of a heavenly body

eclipse (ee KLIHPS) a partial or complete darkening of one heavenly body by another when both line up with the sun or another star

Fahrenheit (FER un hyt) a scale for measuring temperature on which 32 degrees is the freezing point and 212 degrees is the boiling point of water

meteor (MEET ee or) a mass of rock or metal, that enters the earth's atmosphere from space and usually burns up. A meteor that reaches the earth's surface is called a meteorite.

orbit (OR biht) the path that the moon travels around the earth or the earth travels around the sun

phase (fayz) one of several appearances or stages of a thing, like the moon

solar system (SOH lur SIHS tum) the sun and all the planets, moons, and other bodies that move around it